170 Pages of Life

Also by Amna Dhanani

• *My Existence Craves Yours*

• *You were the Soul to my Existence*

• *Phases of Lily*

170 Pages of Life

Amna Dhanani

www.amnadhanani.com
Instagram: **amna_dhanani**
Facebook page: **amnadhanani/**
Youtube: **Amna Dhanani**

Cover vision by **Amna Dhanani**
Brought to life by **Sabinaka**
Editing by **S. H. Kazmi**

About the book

The peacock sheds its feathers every year
and just like that, we shed our old-self
through our experiences into a new-self
throughout our life. While we may shed or
keep many bad and good qualities, one
thing cannot be denied that we learn
through the process each time. So, I chose
to gather the fallen and the new feathers
from my life and decided to compile them
in a book to spread awareness and share a
deep insight.

170 pages of life is a collection of prose
and poetry with constructive perspectives
from many different walks of life.

It has a bonus chapter which has
changed my life forever and if you
follow through, I guarantee, it will
change yours too.

I thank Allah for the pain today,
For it made me realize,
The taste of healing,
Is sweeter than honey.

<u>Never Lose Yourself</u>

Whoever you've lost in your life, losing yourself over them should never be the outcome.

Self-care

It's not about if life has been kind to you,
it's about if you've been kind to yourself.

Meaning of Friendship

Learn the difference
Between friendship and toxicity.
If they *sometimes* treat you good,
That's worse than having no friends.

A friend isn't meant to haunt you at night
and make you weep wondering if they are
really your friend or not.
A friend ruins their sleep if you can't sleep
and wipes your tears.

Leave

For the sake of those nights when your
pillow never dried and you put your arms
around yourself, cradling yourself to sleep,
let that person go and move on.

That person can be a mother who
abandoned you, an ex who cheated on you
or a best friend who stabbed you in the
back. They aren't worth it, you paid your
dues, you know, they don't deserve you.

Apathy

People can't sympathize with pain that they haven't endured, they'll try but it'll sound like the moth is suddenly attracted to the sun instead of the flame, as if your pain doesn't matter because the whole world aches.

Be Your Own Sun

One of the worst mistakes you can make is
let your world revolve around someone
else's.

And this goes for every relationship in your
life whether it's your parents, your spouse,
your children or your friends.

There is a proper way to dedicate your life
to others. It has nothing to do with
revolving around them.

Closed Doors

Some doors have to be closed abruptly
to stay shut.

Reminder #1

There's no substitute for a physical presence. Don't lose the ones around you for the ones far away.

Kindness 101

There's a right way to do the right thing.
Just because your intentions were good
doesn't mean your actions were too.

The Right Action

It's not always about who is right and who is wrong, if someone gets hurt, they deserve an apology.

Apology

If an apology starts with **if**, it's not an apology.

Crocodile Tears

Crying eyes don't lie
unless it's the lying eyes that cry.

Irony

Our intentions are often questioned by
those who claim to know us.

A Better Place

If you want to make a difference in the world, you don't need millions, a smile as kindness is enough.

Reminder #2

Passion is one of the things that feed our
souls.
Don't ever give up on it.

Unapologetic

Self-love is doing right by yourself without feeling apologetic.

Learning

Life is the name of constantly learning
how to appreciate what you have
and let go of what you don't.

Purpose

New paths may remain undiscovered
if we don't get lost.

– Feeling lost has a purpose as well

Love

You shouldn't have to ask for love.

Responsibility

Before you rush into a relationship, make sure you are able to give back what you desire for yourself.

<u>Humanity</u>

We make mistakes because we are human.
Now to remain human, we must try to
correct them as well.

Keepsake

There are two things you will remember the
most in your life:

Teachings from the wise
And lessons from the unwise.

Reminder #3

Sometimes we focus on the definition of love so much that we forget, it's kindness more than anything else.

Willingness

You don't get okay by thinking you have to
but by thinking that you want to. The way
you think matters, even if there's no choice
but to be okay.

<u>Kindness</u>

Kindness begins with the way you think.
Be kind to others inside your head as you
would if you were talking out loud.

Reminder #4

Nothing looks after you more than your hope, don't lose it.

Blank Pages

Some chapters in our lives remain
incomplete and we refuse to believe it's the
end but there cannot be a more certain
proof of a goodbye other than blank pages.

Reminder #5

Friends and family are supposed to make you feel better, not worse. Always remember that.

<u>Wisdom</u>

An ocean isn't considered deep just because of its depth but because of what it contains in the depth.

<u>Unjust</u>

Just because you understand it,
doesn't make it fair to you.

Positive Outlook

Pain bleeds hope
whether you see it that way or not.

Be True to Yourself

They will judge you even if you don't do anything. Just do what you think is right and keep your intentions real.

<u>Courage</u>

If softness were weakness,
the flowers would never grow.

The Circle of Life

Sometimes they don't deserve the healing
they receive from you but often, we become
a medium for someone else's needs.

Self-respect

Don't lose your self-respect for anyone because ironically, the one you will be making this huge sacrifice for, will leave you for not having it.

Reminder #6

Stay away from two kinds of people at all
costs.

Those who are used to winning
And those who are used to not winning.

The first one will suck your energy even in
small arguments and the second one will
leave you completely drained because
you'll keep trying to make them at least try
but they won't.

Tragedy

We've learned to do such a good job at
pretending to be happy that when we really
are happy, we don't know how to react.

Exit

It's time to leave when their silence doesn't break you but their words do.

Difference

There's a difference between tired and
weak,
learn it before you call someone weak.

Depth

There's no depth in one's soul without compassion.

Hesitation

The pauses before a yes and a no have more
meaning than those words could ever hold.

Arrogance

Arrogance finds home in unforgiving
hearts.

Unfortunate

So many good faces are wasted with an
arrogant soul.

Chaos

We live lies and seek the truth
and then wonder, why the world is in chaos.

Amna Dhanani

Witness

If you've witnessed someone's pain,
you should feel honored to have been
chosen
because they've let you see it for a reason.
Someone's pain is one of those ugly scars
no one wants anyone to find out
and they chose you to witness it.

If someone has witnessed your pain,
you should feel grateful,
for there are so many people in the world
who don't even have anyone to witness
their happiness
and be proud of yourself
for being brave enough to let it out.

Choice

Life does not happen at birth, you make it happen when you realize what do you want out of being born.

<u>You</u>

Love heals but it isn't the cure, you are.

Attacker

If you use truth as a weapon and deliver it with rudeness, you're not honest, you're an attacker.

Truth is important but so is kindness. You cannot keep one and forget the other.

<u>Empty</u>

When all they do is take is when they will
find themselves to be empty.

Love Yourself

Reassure and validate your feelings so that you won't expect it from others.

Amna Dhanani

Fate

The good that you think you deserve
comes to you when you actually deserve it.

Denial

They do not believe what they have not experienced.

Amna Dhanani

Self-control

Sometimes we have to bear wrongdoings in order to not do something bad ourselves in haste.

Point of View

They say, the best are those who help
others.
I say, the best are those who are humans to
other humans.

<u>Observation</u>

We often use the word hate for the things
we are afraid of.

Reminder #7

Never settle for anything less than
kindness, especially in a partner.

Essential

Someone who respects you, won't make a fool out of you for wanting the basics in life.

Journey

It's the walk that matters, not the shoes.

Reassurance

Troubled minds are like lost children.
They both need reassurance before
guidance.

Contentment

To feel fulfilled, we have to add value
to what we do or do what we value.

The One

Life isn't about your first love,
it's about the love of your life.

Reminder #8

When you meet someone for the first time
and something feels off, it's because it
usually is. Trust your gut and don't wait to
see if they're good or not because everyone
has a nice side.

Priorities

Getting yourself back together is harder
than finding love again. Don't let others
break you, don't lose yourself.

The Wrong Reason

If you're only being with someone so
you're not left alone, you will be left alone.

We All Are Human

We can be good but not perfect.
When someone close to you hurts you,
remember that.

<u>Be Yourself</u>

Changing yourself over someone's opinion
is like fixing something that isn't broken.

Phony World

It's become almost impossible to find those
who are who they say they are.

The Truth

There is no right or wrong.
The truth is subjective.
Experiences differ.
And then there's simply ignorance.

– Just my opinion about opinions

Red Flags

We tend to ignore red flags because we desperately need to believe humanity still exists.

You for Yourself

If the state of your being, your heart, your mind and your soul does not matter to you, it will not matter to anyone else. And if by a rare chance it does, it will be of no use. For one can help you get up, staying up is your choice alone.

Move on

Forgive them for not being
what they weren't meant to be.

You Deserve Better

I'm sure they deserved it but you didn't deserve to give it to them.

You didn't deserve to put stains on your soul for them.

Amna Dhanani

Share

Sometimes when we don't talk about it, we
don't even realize how much we are hurting
and in how many ways.

Living

Healing means you don't have to force
yourself to live anymore.

Kind Stranger

You don't have to be everyone's saviour,
just be a kind stranger.

<u>Existence</u>

We've lived for too long
but how little we've lived.

<u>Solitude</u>

If you've found peace in solitude,
then you've won.

Fact

Forever is an illusion, love isn't.

Reminder #9

You can't please everyone even if you were perfect because then, they would envy you.

<u>Moving on</u>

Moving on is not a race, it's a process.
It's okay to take your time.

Efforts

Efforts don't need to have results in order
to qualify as efforts.

Worth

Sometimes the tears in someone else's eyes
for you introduce you to your own value.

<u>Voice</u>

Don't lose your voice because of a few deaf
ears.

Let Go

Never beg anyone to stay because even if
they did, it would be out of pity not love.

Mental Health

People who are bad for your mental health
don't have to be bad in general. You've got
to do what is best for you and stay away.

Live Unapologetically

Keep your tone unapologetic. They should not be able to put you to guilt for the things you know are right. Stand your ground.

– Don't let them make you doubt yourself

Reminder #10

The wise aren't wise about everything yet.

<u>Bully</u>

There are so many bullies are hiding behind their white hair.

Amna Dhanani

Full Circle

The very breath we take is a pure example
of what comes has to go.

Reminder #11

Those who always advise us cannot always give us the best advice.

Real Face

Some people show their real face not when you are at your low but when they are at their high.

Reminder #12

Do not make appreciation a matter of validation.

Amna Dhanani

Reward

Wounded become wise.

Everything has a purpose, pain does too.
Let's try to not null that purpose as not
every wound becomes a source of wisdom.

Understanding

Inside us, there's a child who just wants a little understanding, that's all.

Amna Dhanani

Harsh Reality

Half of our lives are spent trying to make
things last which aren't supposed to last.

The Right Time

Don't worry about the blessings
Which stopped on their way to you.
The ones meant for you, sooner or later,
Will come all the way through.

Validation

The validation that doesn't come from you
to yourself is always secondhand.

Consequences

If you hurt someone's heart, you might end
up corrupting your own. Kindness saves
you as well, not just them.

Reminder #13

Don't get yourself involved with someone else's opinion of you. They've led a different life, their perception is different. You should not expect words which aren't in their vocabulary. The best way to change their opinion about you, is for you to accept yourself instead of chasing their acceptance.

Toxicity

Some people won't like you just because you don't bend your will to the sound of their voice.

Take Responsibility

Your parents are responsible for what they didn't teach you, not for what you chose not to learn from them. You're to blame for your own actions.

Reminder #14

Some people will deliberately choose to be cruel to your vulnerability. Do not let this stop you from sharing with those who truly care about you. You deserve to get heard by those who know that vulnerability is to be appreciated, respected and admired for the strength it is, not the other way around. And someone who does not do that, especially while being aware of what it took out of you to share with them, they do not deserve anything from you, not even a word but your back turned on them as a response.

<u>Realization</u>

We know a lot of things for a fact but
sometimes, we learn them later.

Treasure

In this era, when you can't be sure of anyone's intentions with you, if you find sincerity in someone who genuinely cares for you, don't take them for granted, because then you will be throwing away something that is purer than gold.

<u>Value</u>

Bring quality to the table and worry less about how many people might or might not join.

Don't sabotage your quality for likeability.

<u>Desire</u>

Until your soul gets what it desires, other joys of this world become a temporary escape.

Unacceptable

Don't scratch someone's wounds to see
what lies underneath. Just because you
don't understand their pain doesn't give
you a permission to dig until your curiosity
is satisfied.

Catastrophe

There's nothing more tragic for humanity
when one stops being kind because the
world has not been kind to them.

Amna Dhanani

The Blame Game

You're made of your parents' upbringing,
your circumstances, your perspective on
life, your social circle, whatever you went
through and your actions.

You cannot blame yourself, anyone else or
circumstances every time something bad
happens, it's illogical.

109

Reminder #15

Self-care isn't being selfish.
Being selfish isn't self-care.

Read that again.

Ironic

Those who say sorry all the time, don't say
it when they should.

Reminder #16

If it's meant to be, it will happen.
Let the belief take over you, not the fear.

<u>Growth</u>

Real progress is made gradually.
There's no shortcut or a simple answer.
It's all about practice and patience.

<u>Necessity</u>

Break the ties
which are broken from the other side.

Wealth

If your soul is poor, the diamonds of this
world won't make you rich.

– One of the jewels for the soul is kindness.

Power and Wisdom

True wisdom is to know when to get away from a situation which was meant to drain you completely. True power is to be able to do it unaffectedly.

Reminder #17

If you can't find the solution to a problem,
the only solution for the time being is to not
dwell in it.

Intrusion

You don't owe anyone answers of the questions they shouldn't have asked in the first place.

Reminder #18

Don't give something hard the label of
cannot.

Play Your Part

Even if you know what your partner means,
let them tell you and explain in their words.
Don't be a translator of their actions,
otherwise, you will always starve for
efforts.

– Play your part and let them play theirs

Reminder #19

In the sea,
you don't try to tame the wild waves,
you turn your boat away.
Same should be done with anger.

Certainty

Never doubt yourself when you are certain
about something. Go for it even if there is a
chance that things might go south.
Because you are blessed with certainty
which is rarer than love.

Reminder #20

Someone who does not accept your past,
shouldn't be your future.

The Real Strength

Vulnerability is not a sign of weakness.
The sun is vulnerable twice a day for
everyone to look at it,
But it's still powerful enough to burn
anything that gets too close.

Reminder #21

Your past became past for a reason,
Keep moving forward.

Thin Line

There's a thin line between hope and expectation.

Reminder #22

In this era of agony,
I hope you choose to be kind
Even if it's in form of just a smile.
In this era of sin,
I hope you choose
To stay true to your morals.
In this era of hate,
I hope you choose to give out
As much love as you can carry,
Even if it's just a bigger piece of the cake.
In this era of destruction,
I hope you choose forgiveness,
As it takes a lot more courage
To forgive than taking revenge.
In this era, when no one is anyone's
anybody,
I hope you choose to be there
For those who always are there for you,
And won't take them for granted.

<u>Strive</u>

Time cannot heal you without your efforts.

Reminder #23

The love that makes you question if it's love or not, isn't love.

<u>Outlook</u>

An opened book is useless for a closed mind.

Salt

Society is salt for our wounds.
They tell you, you should've known better
rather than admitting what the other person
did was wrong.

Reminder #24

Don't ask anyone the questions that make
you think less of yourself.

Acceptance

Accept people accepting you,
don't push them away.

Merit

Self-harm isn't only done on our body but on our mind as well, when we refuse to believe our own worth.

The Becoming

We have to constantly accept ourselves as who we were, who we are and who we are becoming. Especially when nothing makes sense in the becoming.

Vital

Connect with humanity more than humans.

Connection

One must not take their connection with
themselves for granted.

Trust

Someone who makes you second guess
everything isn't worth your trust.

Ugly Trait

An unforgiving heart is a venomous snake,
which bites its own flesh.

Rare Trait

The ability to forgive and forget is rare.

I know a lot of people believe that we must not forget after forgiving, because how else are we to learn the lesson all this happened in the first place for?

Let me tell you how I see things.
As most of us might already be aware that forgiving does not mean giving a second chance, it simply means that we refuse to keep hatred and resentment in our hearts for anyone or anything.
We are freeing ourselves of the hurt caused by others. I believe in this process, we have to forget what was done as well. We need to put the past behind us in order to be healed completely, I believe that is how we can refuse to suffer by the aftermath of the whole ordeal.

This process differs from person to person though. For some, that is possible after they've healed and for others, it's supposed to happen in order for them to heal.

Again, it's easier said than done but that's what life is all about. It's not possible to not be hurt whether you keep your heart open or not because a closed heart hurts as well, the difference is, there's a denial when it's closed.

Expectations

Sometimes we don't realize we've been
trying to live up to someone's expectations
until we stop doing it.

Reflect

Don't think bad about others, it won't undo
what bad they might've done but you might
end up corrupting your heart.

Amna Dhanani

Boundaries

Don't let anyone cross your boundaries just because they've been good to you.

143

Termite

A doubt is capable of eating up your whole life without burping.

Doubt

Doubting others' intentions can harden your heart.

Period

Don't blame love
For what people did to you.

The Process

If it hurts, let it hurt.
If it heals, let it heal.
Don't try to stop the process,
You will only delay it.

Reminder #25

The process cannot be rushed. If you run
out of time, then it was all you were meant
to learn.

<u>Certitude</u>

If your speech isn't kind
Your generosity means nothing.

Wonders

Your wonders may be small but they are
still wonders.

Reminder #26

Sometimes it's okay to give up on people who can but won't change for better. They need to learn and grow on their own.

Hypocrisy

Isn't it hypocrisy to expect others to accept
us when we don't accept ourselves?

Unheard

Some people are so unheard that they even
take your turn to speak.

Present

Sometimes you have to become better instead of waiting for a better time.

Reminder #27

Sometimes unsolicited advice makes you
look bad even if you meant good.

Mindfulness

There's a thin line between sharing
something bad that happened to you and
backbiting the person who did it to you.

Golden Fruit

Your patience will be as fruitful as you
choose it to be.

What Makes Us Human

A man who is not humble is not a humble man but a man who is not kind isn't a man.

Amna Dhanani

Mind Games

Some pretend to not understand where they went wrong just so they can get away with it.

159

Overthinking

When we overthink, we restrain ourselves
from ourselves by refusing to hear what we
actually have to say but instead, we dwell
in a circle of pain, by thinking, there's no
way out.

Amna Dhanani

<u>Reminder #28</u>

Sometimes you need strength, not closure.

Amna Dhanani

<u>Reminder #28</u>

Sometimes you need strength, not closure.

Impact

Our voice is a powerful tool we use every day without thinking what kind of impact it makes, good or bad.

Well Played

Sometimes disappointment has nothing to do with expectations but with what came without expecting anything at all.

Patience

If you're patient enough,
You can learn from disagreements.

<u>Baggage</u>

It's upon you to take responsibility of your baggage. What should or should not be taken off is your decision, nobody else's nor can they do it for you.

Change

Don't hate yourself for the things you can change gradually.

Reminder #29

Nothing is too silly or small to share if it
hurts you inside.

What You Feel Matters

In our society, we are taught to be quiet
more than we are taught to speak against
injustice.

Which is what our *deen* teaches us but since
we don't have any guidance and have to
learn by ourselves how to speak up, we end
up learning the wrong way.

The intentions are right but we get carried
away because we've been wronged our
entire lives.

We speak up more than we should.
We speak up on small matters that
should've been disregarded.
We speak up so often that our words start to
have less value.
They don't make the desired impact and
that either worsens our ways of getting
heard or we get silenced and feel there is no
way out.

Because there's no balance.

I wish we were taught the right values
growing up.
I wish we were taught how to balance.
I wish we were taught both sides of the
coin, when to speak up and when to have
patience.

The Last Reminder

A reminder about reminders.

Reminders do nothing unless you feel them,
let them sink in and apply them to your life.
People will keep telling you you're worthy
of love and it won't have any effect on you
unless you start believing it yourself.

A message for those who are struggling.

I will never know your struggles personally
but I assure you, we all are in this together.

To everyone who has been through
unspoken tragedies,
I believe you.

To everyone who sits quietly in the back of
a room while everyone else is enjoying,
I see you.

To everyone who cries when the world is
asleep,
I hear you.

To everyone who is going through pain,
I feel you.

To everyone who is reading this,
You are not alone.
It isn't your fault.
You are not weak for crying.
You matter.
You do deserve love and happiness.
You can do it.
You are beautiful inside and out just the
way you are.

I'm sending my love to you all. ♥

Bonus Chapter

What to do when you feel dead inside?

Disclaimer: This article is not permitted to be published/posted online or offline in any form other than the author herself.

When we feel dead inside, everything starts to feel empty, nothing gives us joy or hope anymore, it happens when we stop growing and it feels like it's the end but it is not.

If you feel dead inside, look around yourself, look at every aspect of your life, and ask yourself,
Are you growing emotionally, mentally, physically, intellectually, in career and business, in relationships, in friendships and most importantly, are you growing spiritually?

You have to really question yourself, what aspect of your life does not fulfill you anymore?
What is it that makes you feel dead inside?
And before you answer, remember, it's upon you to change your state, you cannot depend on somebody else to start loving you or to solve your problems for you.
To get out of this phase, you need to understand one fact that, ultimately, you are your own saviour and you are your own

villain. You have to decide what do you want to be for yourself.

And if the answer you come up with is no, you're not growing in a particular aspect, ask yourself.
"What can I do in order to turn it into a yes?"
"Do I need to change something?"
"Do I need to change how I behave or act around it?"
"Do I have to let something go?"
"Is it a dead end? If yes, am I holding onto it unnecessarily?"

These questions are to give an example, the real question of betterment depends on your circumstances.

And if the answer is that you have to let go of dead relations, friendships or dreams.
I wouldn't say that you end it immediately, I would ask you to ask the questions mentioned above and see, if anything can be done about it but if there's nothing you can do,
then please, do not drag yourself around old decisions that used to make you happy.
And if you still don't wish to move on from them, ask yourself, is it worth it? Is it really worth feeling dead while you're still breathing?

170 Pages of Life

Is it still worth wasting more time on it, the time that you could use to heal and then later on, be happy.

Now when you start asking these questions, you might not know the answer to some. If that happens, please know that there's nothing shameful about not understanding a part of your life. We all go through some phases which make us unable to comprehend a lot about ourselves.

In such circumstances, we can ask ourselves,
 "How can I learn more about myself and my life in this aspect?" And take it from there.

Understanding and knowing yourself more and on a deeper level is the first step towards feeling alive again.
The second step is small changes.
The third step is consistency.
If you hold onto these three, you will start to bloom again.

Now, this is something that takes a lot of time. It's not an immediate solution, I guess there are hardly any immediate solutions to what matters the most.
But this is better than doing nothing about your state.
A quality life is built gradually and nothing good in it can be rushed.

Amna Dhanani

How to get out of the loop of negative emotions by asking yourself

"Why, What, How and When"

There are many times in our life when we feel stuck. It often happens when our usual solutions stop working and it's normal to feel negative at this time but when we keep feeling one negative emotion, it leads to thinking about it and thinking about it leads to feeling many negative emotions.

Now, everyone knows that negative emotions make us take negative actions, for example, we start to run away from our feelings, distract or numb ourselves which is very easy to do in today's world.
It helps momentarily but it does not fix anything, the problem stays there whether you choose to look at it or not.
Another behaviour that has become very common nowadays is to wait for the time to get better, for things to get better on their own. We keep delaying the action needed and when this becomes a habit, a negative loops starts to make its place in our life.

As Thomas Watson has said *"The ability to ask the right question is more than half the battle of finding the answer."*

Today, I'm going to tell you a constructive chain of questions that will form up the appropriate actions that have helped me turn my life around for the better, I guarantee you, if you follow through, it will do the same for you.

Step 1: Take a pen and a notebook. You can easily use your phone or laptop for this. You're going to write four questions with their answers.

Step 2: Now focus on one negative feeling that you constantly feel and write it down as the title.

Step 3: Ask yourself "Why do you feel the way you do?" And write down this question

In this step, you must face your issue or issues. It may take a while but write down every reason for that feeling to come up again and again. For example, if you're feeling tired physically or mentally, cover every topic that makes you feel this way. This may vary from small tasks like washing dishes to heavy tasks such as having excessive homework every day. Just make a list of everything that comes to your mind.

Step 4: Pick one topic from the list and write it down on a separate page as a title.

Step 5: Ask yourself "What can you do to fix this?" And write down this question.

Again, take your time and write down everything that you can think of that may help whether you've tried it before or not. In this step, you must challenge yourself to think how to make it better for yourself. Let's take the previous example, if you're tired of washing dishes, what can you do to make your experience better? Or what can you do to lessen your burden so that you may feel less tired?

Option A: You can request your roommate or any one in your family to do it for you for a day, so that you may be able to relax. (This is a temporary fix)

Option B: You can hire a maid. (This is a long term fix, if you can afford)

Option C: You can request every person who uses the dishes, to wash the one they use, so that you will only have to wash the ones you use. (This is a lifetime fix as it can be made into a good habit for generations)

Right here, I would like to mention that every problem can have many solutions and

while it might seem very natural to go for a lifetime fix, it's not as easy as the other two options.
You can work from the easiest solution to the hardest one for your personal growth. Again, as we all know, change is the key to growth, being still benefits nobody.

I've mentioned 3 options that came to my mind but the possibilities to tackle our situations are endless. Once we start writing down, our mind automatically searches for possibilities and ways to take care of what is at hand. You might come up with solutions that you have never even thought of before.

No matter how big or small what you're facing is, there's always a way out even if there seem to be none.
Our mind registers everything we write. So by writing down what you're feeling, you're acknowledging it on a deeper level. By writing down what you can do, you're learning what your physical obstacles are and how you can tackle them. By writing down solutions, you're gaining an insight to what so many people are not conscious of in day to day life. And by writing all of this down, you're already getting on top of your game.

You're facing the problem

Amna Dhanani

You're thinking productively
about how to solve it,
Your mind is processing,
Your heart is into it,
Your body is feeling that energy.

Step 6: Choose one of the options that you
think you can work with right now and
write it down on a separate page as a title.

Step 7: Ask yourself "How do I take actions
for what I want to do?" And write down
this question.

If you choose option A, write down how
would you ask the other person to do the
dishes.

If you choose option B, write down how
can you hire a maid, for example, asking
your neighbours et cetera.

Step 8: Ask yourself "When would be the
right time to execute the plan you've just
made?" And write down this question.

It seems that the answer to this question
would be simple but it's not.
For example, you cannot ring your
neighbour's doorbell at 2 am in the morning
to ask how they hired their maid! That
would be a little coo-coo.

So you wait until the next day, but when you are so used to procrastinating, you're more likely to delay the action than it requires.

So the right answer to this question is, the right action at the right time.

There you go! You have now fixed one problem that made you feel tired, you can take others out one by one! Step by step or even write your plan by breaking it into many small goals. In my personal experience, making and achieving small goals is most effective.

There is no restriction here. You may work with your pace and do a step each day or do one topic each day. It all depends on you. You can create healthy habits out of achieving your goals and when one plan is done, you can create another plan. With consistency, you will see great results gradually just by asking yourself the right questions.

And lastly, I want you to ask yourself the most important question, are you appreciating yourself for this absolutely amazing progress?

Reading this article till the end is a great progress, please pat yourself on the shoulder for me!

In my debut poetry book
'My Existence Craves Yours'
There's this piece I added *"There are so many feelings I want to share with the world but I'm afraid that they won't reach the souls in need."*

One day, I found a quote in a random book I was reading, it answered a question I had had for a long time. That day, I realized there have been many times this has happened to me as well, I realized that the souls in need are automatically directed towards the words they need to hear, when they need to hear it, whether it's from someone's mouth, a book or other million ways. This realization has changed my personal and my career life both. I hope this little miracle helps you too.

Please consider leaving a review on
Amazon
and Goodreads.
A few words will help tremendously ♥

About the Author

Amna Dhanani, now a world-renowned author, hails from a small town in Sindh, Pakistan. Her journey started when she was 11 with an article she wrote inspired by her mother. The praise she received for this article gave birth to a writer in her with the sole purpose of touching souls.

Amna has only attended school till 8th grade; however, her passion to learn and pursue the creative journey has paved the way for her. She is self-taught, passionate and a diligent writer who has specialized the art of speaking volumes in a few words.

Her keen observation of the world is the reason she has been able to stand against the unjust norms in the society. She is now breaking stereotypes and speaking about topics that are left undiscussed. In her three poetry books, 'My Existence Craves Yours', 'You were the Soul to My Existence' and 'Phases of Lily', she talks about her perception of various shades of this world including love, pain, mental health and heartbreaks of many kinds. Not only that, but Amna has become a voice for those who struggle and teaches the wisdom required for survival.

www.ingramcontent.com/pod-product-compliance
Lightning Source LLC
Chambersburg PA
CBHW030828090426
42737CB00009B/928